VOLCANOES

by Lauren Coss

Content Consultant
Jennifer Rivers Cole, PhD
Department of Earth & Planetary Sciences

CORE

Printed in the United States of America,
North Mankato, Minnesota
042013
1102013

THIS BOOK CONTAINS AT LEAST 10% RECYCLED MATERIALS.

Editor: Mirella Maxwell
Series Designer: Becky Daum

Library of Congress Control Number: 2013932503

Cataloging-in-Publication Data
Coss, Lauren.
 Volcanoes / Lauren Coss.
   p. cm. -- (Earth in action)
ISBN 978-1-61783-942-9 (lib. bdg.)
ISBN 978-1-62403-007-9 (pbk.)
1. Volcanoes--Juvenile literature. 2. Natural disasters--Juvenile literature. I. Title.
551.21--dc23

                                   2013932503

Photo Credits: Shutterstock Images, cover, 1, 39; USGS Cascades Volcano Observatory/Harry Glicken/AP Images, 4; Jack Smith/AP Images, 6, 10; Austin Post/U.S. Geological Survey, 9; Ammit Jack/Shutterstock Images, 12; U.S. Geological Survey, 14, 45; John T. Takai/Shutterstock Images, 17; Andrea Danti/Shutterstock Images, 18; iStockphoto/Thinkstock, 20, 23; George W. Bailey/Shutterstock Images, 24; Al Grillo/AP Images, 26; Bullit Marquez/AP Images, 28; Itsuo Inouye/AP Images, 31; Erwin Patzelt/picture-alliance/dpa/AP Images, 34; Zack Frank/Shutterstock Images, 37; Marco Ugarte/AP Images, 40

CONTENTS

CHAPTER ONE
A Mountain Explodes 4

CHAPTER TWO
The Fire Within 14

CHAPTER THREE
Eruption! 20

CHAPTER FOUR
Taking a Volcano's Pulse 28

CHAPTER FIVE
A Fiery Future 34

Ten Amazing Volcanic Eruptions 42

Stop and Think 44

Glossary 46

Learn More 47

Index 48

About the Author 48

A MOUNTAIN EXPLODES

The spring of 1980 was uneasy for people living near Mount Saint Helens in Washington. They were waiting for a big event to happen. Mount Saint Helens's summit, or peak, stood at 9,677 feet (2,950 m). It was a popular place for hiking, fishing, climbing, and camping. But on May 18, 1980, the forest around the mountain was unusually quiet.

Mount Saint Helens is photographed on May 17, 1980. The mountain had little activity in the few days before the major explosion.

In the first few days of activity, Mount Saint Helens blew ice and rock from many of its craters.

Warning Signs

A few months earlier, a series of small earthquakes shook the mountain. Before that time, Mount Saint Helens had been quiet for decades. Scientists began paying attention. On March 27, 1980, Mount Saint Helens erupted for the first time in 123 years. It was a small eruption, but the blast was so powerful it blew a hole in the mountain.

Authorities evacuated hundreds of people living and working near Mount Saint Helens. Many residents were unhappy about leaving. Scientists watching the volcano feared the worst was still to come. A large bulge had formed on the northern side of the mountain. Scientists believed magma inside the mountain was pushing toward the mountain's peak. The magma was causing the bulge to swell at a rate of nearly six and a half feet (2 m) a day. Small eruptions and earthquakes continued for weeks. The volcano kept growing, and by mid-May, the bulge had grown 450 feet (137 m) outward from the volcano. Then one day, activity on the volcano seemed to stop. Scientists wondered if the worst was over.

Lava or Magma?

Magma is hot, liquid rock deep inside Earth. This magma escapes to the surface in a volcanic eruption. When the magma reaches the surface, it becomes lava.

"Vancouver, Vancouver! This is it!"

On May 18, 1980, at 8:32 a.m., scientists in Vancouver, Washington, received a frightening call from scientist David Johnston. He said: "Vancouver, Vancouver! This is it!" Another earthquake had rocked the mountain. This time the giant bulge collapsed, and the side of the mountain slid away. The slide created the largest avalanche in recorded history and triggered a volcanic explosion.

A 15-mile (24-km) high cloud of rocks, ash, lava, gas, and steam hurtled out from the volcano at more than 300 miles per hour (480 km/h). The hot materials melted snow and ice at the top of the volcano. The melted water mixed with debris and ash. This formed dangerous mudflows called lahars. The lahars raced into the valley below, destroying everything in their path. Johnston had been watching the volcano from a post about 5 miles (8 km) away. Within moments, the hot volcanic debris ruined his trailer. He was killed instantly.

Mount Saint Helens's enormous eruption on May 18 sent volcanic debris flying in every direction.

Mount Saint Helens did tremendous damage to both land and homes.

Eruptions continued throughout the day. The sky grew dark with ash and debris. By evening on May 18, Mount Saint Helens finally quieted. By that time, the mountain was 1,314 feet (401 m) shorter. Its north side was completely blown away by the volcano. Trees were knocked down for hundreds of miles. Fifty-seven people were killed in the eruption and almost 200 homes were damaged or destroyed. It was the worst US volcanic eruption in more than 60 years.

A Fiery Planet

Mount Saint Helens is one of more than 1,500 active volcanoes around the world. Volcanoes exist on every continent, including Antarctica. They come in all shapes and sizes. Some volcanic eruptions have destroyed entire cities. Other eruptions happen so slowly, a baby could crawl faster than the lava flow. Scientists work hard to study the way volcanoes behave. They want to learn more

Mount Saint Helens Today

Since its 1980 eruption, Mount Saint Helens has become a popular tourist site. New plants grew between the fallen trees, and animals returned to the mountain. More than two decades later in 2004, Mount Saint Helens had a series of small eruptions. A dome of lava formed inside the volcano's crater, or mouth. The volcano was rebuilding itself. Four years later, the mountain grew quiet again. Residents and scientists wonder if Mount Saint Helens is gearing up for its next big eruption.

Volcanoes can be found across the globe. Although they are dangerous, volcanoes are an important part of Earth.

about volcanoes so they can predict the next big eruption.

Volcanoes are an important part of Earth's geology. They have formed much of the land we use today. New land is still forming in some places as a result of volcanic activity. Soil rich with volcanic ash is good for growing crops. Our world would be a very different place without volcanoes!

Geologist Keith Stoffel and his wife Dorothy were flying in a small plane over Mount Saint Helens when it erupted. Keith described their experience:

> *Within a matter of seconds. . . . the whole north side of the summit crater began to move. . . . The entire mass began to ripple and churn up. . . . Then the entire north side of the summit began sliding to the north along a deep-seated slide plane. I was amazed and excited . . . that we were watching this landslide of unbelievable proportions. . . . Before we could snap off more than a few pictures, a huge explosion blasted out of the detachment plane. . . . Dorothy saw the southern portion of the summit crater begin to crumble and slide to the north.*

Source: Keith L. Stoffel. "The May 18, 1980, Eruption of Mount St. Helens – A View from the Top." Michael A. Korosec, James G. Rigby, and Keith L. Stoffel. The 1980 Eruption of Mount St. Helens, Washington March 20–May 18, 1980. Washington State Department of Natural Resources, June 1980. PDF. 5. Web. Accessed December 27, 2012.

Consider Your Audience

Read Keith Stoffel's description closely. What type of audience was he trying to reach? Think about how you could adapt Stoffel's information for a different audience, such as your friends or parents. Write a blog post for the new audience. How is your post different or the same?

CHAPTER TWO

THE FIRE WITHIN

On February 20, 1943, a Mexican farmer was working in his cornfield when a strange event happened. A giant crack opened in his farmland, letting out steam and ash. By the next day, the debris erupting from the crack had created a 10-foot (3-m) high volcano. The volcano, which is located in a part of Mexico dotted with many volcanoes, continued growing. Within a year, the volcano was 1,100 feet

Paricutín is the youngest volcano in the Mexican volcano belt. Scientists have studied Paricutín since its birth.

(335 m) tall. Lava from the volcano ruined farmland in the area and destroyed the nearby village of Paricutín, Mexico. The volcano, also called Paricutín, continued erupting until 1952. It was 1,391 feet (424 m) tall. Paricutín was the first volcano scientists were able to watch from birth to death.

Inside Planet Earth

The center of Earth is an extremely hot core. The core is solid at its center with liquid around it. Surrounding the core is the mantle, which is made of very hot, dense rock. The core heats the bottom of the mantle, causing it to rise. The top of the mantle is cooler and denser than

Infant Island

In November 1963, fishermen off the coast of Iceland were surprised to see smoke, steam, and ash shooting out of the ocean. A new island formed by the next day. The volcanic island, called Surtsey, kept erupting until 1967. The little island was 560 feet (171 m) high. Today biologists use the island to study how plants and animals take over and live on brand-new land.

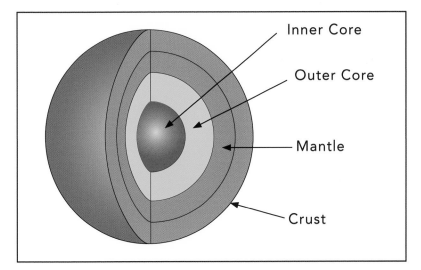

Earth's Interior
This illustration shows the different layers of our planet. Does it look the way you imagined it would when you read the description of Earth's interior? How does this diagram help you understand better how volcanoes form?

the bottom of the mantle, so as the top sinks, it is replaced by the bottom of the mantle.

The crust is the outermost layer of Earth, and it is both cool and solid. It is much less dense than the mantle. The crust is divided into sections called tectonic plates. Tectonic plates move slowly toward or away from each other. Most plates move at the rate of a few inches per year. When tectonic plates move toward each other and collide, subduction zones form. In subduction zones, the denser plate dives

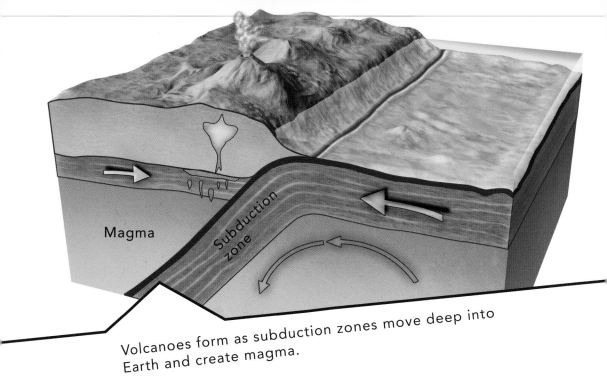

Magma

Subduction zone

Volcanoes form as subduction zones move deep into Earth and create magma.

beneath the less dense plate. As the denser plate drives into Earth, the plate melts from an increase in pressure and temperature. This creates magma, which may rise upward to form volcanoes.

Hot Spots

Some volcanoes are located far from tectonic plate edges. The tallest volcano on Earth, Mauna Loa at 56,000 feet (17,069 m), is a hot spot in the middle of the Pacific Plate. Hot spots are places where a plume of magma is so hot it rises to the surface without cooling.

Mauna Loa is part of the Hawaiian Islands. Scientists think the first Hawaiian island formed when a hot spot slowly built an underwater mountain, which grew to form a volcanic island. The Pacific Plate kept moving, while the hot spot stayed put. The process started over and eventually the Hawaiian Islands formed.

Hawaii's newest island, the Big Island, is still forming. It grows approximately 19 acres (8 ha) per year because of the volcano Kilauea. Kilauea is the most active volcano on Earth, but it is not the most dangerous. The lava is thinner and flows slowly, making it easy for people to move out of its way. This is not the case with all volcanoes. Some volcanoes erupt with enough force and fury to wipe entire cities off the map.

Pele Finds a Home

According to Hawaiian legends, the Hawaiian Islands were built as the goddess Pele searched for a home. Today Pele lives in Kilauea, which is why the volcano is believed to be so active.

CHAPTER THREE

ERUPTION!

The volcano Vesuvius towers over many coastal towns in western Italy. In 79 CE, the bustling Roman city of Pompeii sat six miles (9.7 km) southeast of the volcano. The city of Herculaneum was less than four miles (6.4 km) west of Vesuvius. The volcano had been mostly quiet while Romans lived in the area. Most people did not even realize the peaceful mountain was a volcano.

Mount Vesuvius looms over the ancient city of Pompeii.

On August 24, 79 CE, Vesuvius blew its top. Many people tried to run away, but others stayed behind. They believed it was safest in the shelter of their homes, but they were wrong. The volcano continued erupting until early in the morning of August 25, when Vesuvius's 19-mile (31-km) high ash cloud collapsed. The collapse sent a deadly pyroclastic flow racing into Herculaneum. A pyroclastic flow is a super-hot avalanche of gas, rock, and volcanic debris. It instantly killed the people who stayed in Herculaneum. Another pyroclastic flow swept through Pompeii five hours later, burying the town.

The eruption lasted more than 24 hours. Pompeii was buried under

A Big Eruption

The Indonesian volcano Krakatoa collapsed in 1883. In its largest explosion on August 27, the volcano produced the loudest sound in recorded history. The sound of the blast was heard as far away as Perth, Australia. The volcano also generated a massive tsunami. After the explosion, only two-thirds of the volcano's original island remained.

Although Pompeii was buried in ash for centuries, parts of the city have been excavated and restored. It is a popular tourist spot in Italy.

nine feet (2.7 m) of ash. Herculaneum was covered in 75 feet (23 m) of ash. Both towns remained covered and mostly forgotten for centuries. Pompeii was especially well preserved. Today tourists can visit Pompeii to get a glimpse into the final days of the city.

Mighty Magma

Like other active volcanoes, Vesuvius has a magma chamber. A vent connects the chamber to the

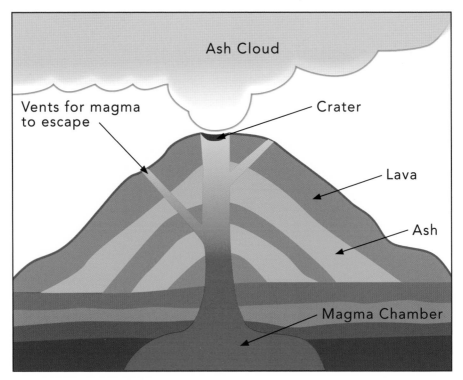

Anatomy of a Volcano
Volcanoes come in many shapes and sizes. But most volcanoes share some characteristics. This diagram shows the main parts of most volcanoes. How does seeing the parts of a volcano help you understand volcanoes better?

volcano's crater. As magma flows into the chamber, pressure in the chamber builds. When there is enough pressure, the volcano erupts.

Some volcanoes, like Vesuvius, have thick magma with a large amount of gas dissolved in the fluid. As the magma rises to the surface, the gas decompresses and is released. This is similar to the way air bubbles escape when a bottle of soda is opened. In volcanoes, the escaping gas causes a huge explosion. Volcanoes with thinner magma and fewer gases often erupt more slowly. Most Hawaiian volcanoes have runny magma. These eruptions are very slow. In most cases, people can safely watch lava flow from a Hawaiian volcano.

The Year without Summer

On April 5, 1815, the Indonesian volcano of Tambora unleashed one of the deadliest eruptions in human history. Its huge cloud of ash circled the entire globe, reflecting sunlight. The average global temperature dropped more than 5 degrees Fahrenheit (3°C) over the next year. In 1816 snow fell in New England as late as June. The European summer was unusually cold and rainy. Many crops failed. It was known as the year without a summer.

Volcanic Dangers

Volcanic eruptions can trigger tsunamis, avalanches, mud slides, and other natural disasters. They may also cause dangerous pyroclastic flows and lahars.

Volcanologists use computer programs and other instruments to monitor volcanic activity. These tools help them better predict future eruptions.

Volcanic eruptions can permanently change the nearby landscape. Some nearby regions are uninhabitable for years. Sometimes a single volcanic eruption can affect the entire world. When the Indonesian volcano of Tambora erupted in 1815, it cooled the northern hemisphere. Many volcanologists, or scientists who specialize in volcanoes, believe future volcanic eruptions could have a similar cooling effect on Earth's climate. Volcanologists spend their lives trying to understand a volcano's next move.

Pliny the Younger witnessed the 79 CE eruption of Pompeii and wrote about the event in his letters:

> *From the other direction . . . a dreadful black cloud was torn by gushing, twisting flames . . . and great tongues of fire. . . . My mother begged me . . . to leave her and escape as best I could. . . . But I told her that I would not save myself without her. . . . Ash was already falling by now, but not very thickly. Then I turned around and saw the thick black cloud advancing over the land behind us like a flood. . . . We had hardly sat down to rest when the darkness fell upon us. But it was not the darkness of a moonless, or cloudy night, but just as if all the lamps had been put out in a completely dark room.*

Source: Alwyn Scarth. *Vulcan's Fury: Man Against the Volcano.* New Haven, CT: Yale UP, 1999. Print. 35.

Nice View

After reading this passage, reread Keith Stoffel's description of the Mount Saint Helens eruption in Chapter One. How is Pliny the Younger's description of the Vesuvius eruption different from Stoffel's description? How are the two authors' points of view the same? Write a short essay comparing Stoffel's and Pliny the Younger's points of view.

TAKING A VOLCANO'S PULSE

In the summer of 1990, the Philippine mountain Pinatubo began to rumble. There was evidence of ancient eruptions, but the volcano had been quiet for centuries. In the spring of 1991, small earthquakes began to shake the Pinatubo area. Nearly 1 million people lived in the mountain's shadow.

Mount Pinatubo awoke in the spring of 1991 and threatened thousands of Philippine citizens.

Watching the Beast

The Philippine government sprang into action, contacting the US Geological Survey (USGS) to help Philippine scientists monitor the volcano. Volcanologists set up seismographs, which are instruments that detect and record earthquakes.

Pinatubo became more violent throughout the spring. Steam explosions blew holes in the volcano, and the mountain emitted smelly sulfur gases. Earthquakes happened more often, and the mountain began to bulge. Scientists saw these events as warning signs. On June 5, 1991, scientists warned a major eruption would likely occur within two weeks. The Philippine

United States Geological Survey

The USGS has a long history of studying Earth. It was established in 1879 to study and monitor natural resources and hazards, including volcanoes. The USGS monitors volcanoes from five observatories located in Alaska, California, Washington, Yellowstone National Park, and Hawaii.

The government and scientists' close monitoring helped save many Philippine citizens, since they were given warning to leave their villages.

government evacuated close to 58,000 people living in the Pinatubo area.

Mount Pinatubo released its first major eruption in recorded history on June 12. Three days later, on June 15, Pinatubo unleashed its largest eruption. A cloud of ash and debris rose 22 miles (35 km) in the air. The sky was completely dark. The ash blanketed the region, collapsing roofs and destroying crops. Pinatubo's summit blew away in the eruption.

Approximately 300 people were killed in the 1991 eruption, but tens of thousands of people were saved thanks to the hard work of the Philippine government and USGS scientists. It was a major victory in eruption prediction.

A Dangerous Science

Studying volcanoes often means getting close to these dangerous mountains. Volcanologists are very careful when they are working near an active volcano. They wear protective gear, such as helmets and heat-resistant clothing. They often wear gas masks to protect their lungs from dangerous fumes. Accidents still happen. Volcanoes kill an average of one volcanologist a year.

Studying Volcanoes

Volcanologists learn more with every new volcanic eruption. They examine the land near volcanoes for evidence of ancient ash falls and pyroclastic flows. Volcanologists try to understand how often a volcano has erupted in its history. This gives a better idea of when a volcano may erupt in the future.

EXPLORE ONLINE

Chapter Four discusses the ways scientists study volcanoes and predict eruptions. Maybe you want to become a volcanologist. Visit the Web site below to learn more about becoming a volcanologist. How does the information in the Web site compare with the information in this chapter? How might the skills discussed on the Web site be used to predict volcanoes?

Information for Future Volcanologists
www.mycorelibrary.com/volcanoes

Volcanologists also look for new gases or liquids coming out of cracks. This may mean magma deep inside the volcano is moving toward the surface.

Volcanologists try to understand how eruptions affect Earth's climate. They look at tree rings and snow layers to learn more about past eruptions. Volcanologists work hard to understand volcanoes and predict eruptions. Volcanoes do not always behave the way scientists expect they will. Even if they suspect a volcano is about to erupt, there is nothing volcanologists can do to stop it.

CHAPTER FIVE

A FIERY FUTURE

Today more than one in twelve people live near an active volcano. Some of these volcanoes could erupt at any time. Other volcanoes might never wake up. Sometimes volcanoes believed to be extinct roar to life. Scientists know of ancient eruptions that have affected the entire planet. Some of these volcanoes are overdue for another eruption.

Some volcanoes have been quiet for centuries, like Licancabur volcano in Chile.

Volcanoes in Space

Some of the biggest volcanoes are out of this world. In fact, the largest known volcano towers above the surface of Mars. This extinct volcano, Olympus Mons, stands 14 miles (23 km) high with a 435-mile (700-km) base. That is almost three times as tall as Mount Everest.

But which one will blow next, and when will the explosion occur?

US Supervolcano

One of the most closely watched volcanoes lies in the United States underneath Yellowstone National Park. Yellowstone sits above a hot spot, which creates the steaming geysers and hot springs in the park. This hot spot also feeds a giant supervolcano. Supervolcanoes are volcanoes that produce huge eruptions. These eruptions are big enough to change the global climate. They often lead to plant and animal extinctions.

An eruption at the Yellowstone hot spot 2 million years ago left a hole in the ground about the size of Rhode Island. Yellowstone's most recent eruption was

Many visitors to Yellowstone National Park are unaware it sits on top of an active volcano. Volcanologists closely monitor this hot spot.

640,000 years ago. Scientists believe this eruption scattered ash all the way to the Gulf of Mexico.

The Yellowstone volcano is still active and growing. Most scientists do not expect an eruption in the near future. But they want to be ready at the first sign the volcano is gearing up to explode.

Vesuvius Again?

Yellowstone is not the only volcano being closely monitored. Some scientists believe Mount Vesuvius is still one of the most dangerous volcanoes on Earth.

More than 3 million people live in the shadow of Vesuvius today. The large city of Naples, Italy, sits just across a bay from the mountain. Scientists believe Vesuvius has a major eruption once every 2,000 years. It has been almost 2,000 years since Vesuvius's last major eruption—the one that buried Pompeii and Herculaneum. A future eruption of Vesuvius could be more deadly than ever before.

Other Dangerous Volcanoes

People pay close attention to other volcanoes around the world. Popocatépetl towers just 40 miles (64 km)

Mount Fuji in Japan sits close to a bustling city. If it were to erupt, it could endanger thousands of people.

away from 18 million people living in Mexico City, Mexico. Merapi in Indonesia frequently ejects lava and ash from its crater. Scenic Mount Fuji in Japan could put 30 million people living in nearby Tokyo in danger if it were to erupt.

Warning systems and evacuation plans are in place for each of these volcanoes. Officials are prepared to act quickly if signs point to a major eruption.

Although volcanoes are dangerous, the land surrounding them is good for crops and animals.

Volcanic Benefits

It may seem strange so many people choose to live near such dangerous volcanoes. When they are not erupting, volcanoes make great places to build cities. Volcanic soil is very rich, and crops grow well. Livestock, such as sheep and cattle, thrive on grasses that grow on former eruption sites.

Volcanoes have helped shape our planet, and they will continue to change Earth's landscape. Volcanoes will always erupt. It is our job to try to understand them. If we pay attention to the warnings they give us, we can learn how to live in harmony with these fiery mountains.

FURTHER EVIDENCE

Chapter Five has a great deal of information about how we view volcanoes today. If you could pick out the main point of the chapter, what would it be? Choose a quote from the Web site below that relates to this chapter. Does this quote support the author's main point, or does it make a new point? Write a few sentences explaining how the quote you found relates to Chapter Five.

Information on Volcanoes

www.mycorelibrary.com/volcanoes

Approximately 74,000 years ago

Mount Toba, Sumatra

Mount Toba erupted approximately 74,000 years ago. It is considered to have changed the global climate for years and may have nearly caused humans to become extinct.

Approximately 3,600 years ago

Santorini, Greece

When Santorini erupted around 3,600 years ago, it blew apart the island where it stood. The blast may have inspired the legend of Atlantis. Today several islands exist on top of the still-active volcano.

79 CE

Vesuvius, Italy

In 79 CE, Mount Vesuvius's last major eruption destroyed Pompeii and Herculaneum. Almost 2,000 years later, some scientists think Vesuvius is preparing to blow again.

April 1815

Tambora, Indonesia

Tambora's most recent eruption was in April 1815. The event led to global climate change, triggering the year without a summer. It was the deadliest recorded volcanic eruption in history.

August 26–27, 1883

Krakatoa, Indonesia

Krakatoa is one of the most famous volcanoes on Earth. Its 1883 eruption was heard for thousands of miles. Only a small part of the original island remained after the explosion.

May 8, 1902

Mount Pelée, Martinique

Mount Pelée is located on the Caribbean Island of Martinique. Its last major eruption was in 1902, when deadly pyroclastic flows wiped out the French colony of St. Pierre. Mount Pelée had another minor eruption in 1929.

June 6–8, 1912
Novarupta, United States
In 1912 the Alaskan volcano Novarupta erupted for 60 hours. It was the largest eruption of the 1900s. The volcano is very isolated, so no lives were lost.

May 18, 1980
Mount Saint Helens, United States
Mount Saint Helens roared to life in the spring of 1980 in one of the largest North American volcano eruptions in history. It is one of the most-studied volcanoes in the world.

June 15, 1991
Pinatubo, Philippines
In 1991 Pinatubo erupted for the first time in 600 years. The eruption left more than 100,000 people homeless. The careful predictions by scientists from the United States and the Philippines saved many lives.

March 20–June 23, 2010
Eyjafjallajökull, Iceland
In the spring of 2010, Eyjafjallajökull captured headlines around the world when it erupted. The ash cloud disrupted air travel across Europe for a week.

Why Do I Care?

This book talks about what happens when a volcano erupts. Maybe you live near an active volcano. If so, how would your life change if the volcano erupted? Even if you live far from volcanoes, they still have an important effect on Earth. How would your life be different if there were no volcanoes? Use your imagination!

You Are There

Chapter Three of this book discusses the eruption of Vesuvius and how it affected Pompeii and Herculaneum. Imagine you are living near Vesuvius in 79 CE. What do you see, hear, and smell? How do you feel about the eruption? What do you do when you see ash rising from Vesuvius?

Say What?

Studying volcanoes can mean learning many new words. Find five words in this book you have never seen or heard before. Use a dictionary to find out what they mean. Then write the meanings in your own words, and use each word in a sentence.

Surprise Me

Learning about volcanoes can be interesting and surprising. What three facts about the volcanoes in this book did you find most surprising? Write a few sentences about each fact. Why did you find these facts surprising?

GLOSSARY

crater
the mouth of a volcano

extinct
no longer active or in existence

lava
super-hot liquid rock at Earth's surface

magma
super-hot liquid rock below Earth's surface

plume
columns of molten rock rising from Earth

pyroclastic flow
a fast-moving avalanche of hot gas, dust, ash, rock, and other volcanic debris triggered when a volcano's ash cloud collapses

seismograph
a machine that measures Earth's movement

summit
the peak of a mountain

supervolcano
a huge and powerful volcano capable of enormous eruptions that can trigger global climate change and plant and animal extinctions

volcanologist
a scientist who specializes in volcanoes

LEARN MORE

Books

Berger, Melvin and Gilda. *Why Do Volcanoes Blow Their Tops?* New York: Scholastic, 2000.

Fradin, Judith and Dennis. *Volcano! The Icelandic Eruption of 2010 and Other Hot, Smoky, Fierce, and Fiery Mountains.* Washington, DC: National Geographic, 2010.

Hamilton, S. L. *Volcanoes.* Minneapolis, MN: ABDO, 2012.

Web Links

To learn more about volcanoes, visit ABDO Publishing Company online at **www.abdopublishing.com.** Web sites about volcanoes are featured on our Book Links page. These links are routinely monitored and updated to provide the most current information available. Visit **www.mycorelibrary.com** for free additional tools for teachers and students.

INDEX

ash, 8, 10, 12, 15, 16, 22–24, 25, 27, 31, 32, 37, 39

core, 16–17
crater, 11, 13, 24, 39
crust, 17

debris, 8, 10, 15, 22, 31

eruption, 6–7, 10–13, 22, 25–27, 29, 30–33, 35, 36–40

Hawaiian Islands, 19
Herculaneum, 21–23, 38

Kilauea, 19
Krakatoa, 22

lahars, 8, 25

lava, 7, 8, 11, 16, 19, 24, 25, 39
lava beds, 38

magma, 7, 18, 23–25, 33
magma chamber, 23, 24
mantle, 16–17
Mauna Loa, 18–19
Mount Fuji, 39
Mount Saint Helens, 5–13, 27
Mount Vesuvius, 21–27, 37–38

Pacific Plate, 18–19
Paricutín, 16
Paricutín, Mexico, 16
peak, 5, 7
Philippines, 29–32
Pinatubo, 29–31
plume, 18
Pompeii, 21–23, 27

Popocatépetl, 38
pyroclastic flow, 22, 25, 32

subduction zones, 17–18
summit, 5, 13, 31
supervolcano, 36–37
Surtsey, 16

Tambora, 25–26
tectonic plates, 17, 18

US Geological Survey (USGS), 30, 32

vent, 23–24
volcanologists, 26, 30, 32–33

Yellowstone National Park, 30, 36–37

ABOUT THE AUTHOR

Lauren Coss is a writer and editor who lives in Saint Paul, Minnesota.